The discipline of a fallen leader' is not a punishment by others. It is a voluntarily accepted role of one who believes the full teaching of the Word about three things: God's mercy in forgiveness, God's summons to restoration and the obligation of every spiritual leader to accept the counsel of other leaders in the spirit of submission.

"That's what 'the discipline of time' is about: healing and mending, not punishment. And the one who accepts that discipline becomes a disciple again, at a fresh point of beginning— forgiven and cleansed, and ready for the process of recovery."

—J.W.H.

JACK W. HAYFORD

Restoring Fallen Leaders

Regal Books

A Division of GL Publications
Ventura, California, U.S.A.

Published by Regal Books
A Division of GL Publications
Ventura, California 93006
Printed in U.S.A.

Library of Congress Cataloging-in-Publication Data applied for.

2 3 4 5 6 7 8 9 10 / 91 90 89

Rights for publishing this book in other languages are contracted by Gospel Literature International (GLINT) foundation. GLINT also provides technical help for the adaptation, translation, and publishing of Bible study resources and books in scores of languages worldwide. For further information, contact GLINT, Post Office Box 488, Rosemead, California, 91770, U.S.A., or the publisher.

DEDICATION

In dedicating this small book to them, I am aware its size is hardly worthy to reflect the wealth of understanding I have received from the lives of "fathers in the faith" whose lives have so impressed, influenced and shaped mine.

I praise God for His grace which allowed me to be taught and guided by the example of these notable pastors and leaders of highest fidelity to the Word of God and deepest integrity in living out that Word.

Dr. Vincent Bird, my first overseer and continuing counselor and friend;

Dr. Kenneth Erickson, though now with Christ his life still influences mine;

Rev. Maurice Tolle, who preached the gospel the night I received Christ, and who still stands as a model of servanthood;

Drs. Guy P. Duffield, Nathaniel Van Cleave, Clarence Hall and Leslie Eno; pastor-teachers all—who pressed me into the Word by their instruction and who kept me there by their example.

PREFACE

Anna and I were en route from Calgary, Alberta to Vancouver, British Columbia. The scenic train route through the Canadian Rockies was fulfilling every expectation—beauty, splendor, grandeur and restfulness. We were being overwhelmed by one panorama after another when we came to the point where our guide observed, "We are now at the Continental Divide." He went on to explain that from the place to which we had presently come, all streams parted. The melting snow on one side of the crest would eventually flow into the Pacific Ocean, and that which was virtually adjacent—but inches away—would arrive in the Atlantic or the Gulf of Mexico months from now.

There is no questioning that an unusual grace has been poured upon the Church during the last several years and, like the sunlit brilliance of snow crowning a mountain range, a glory has accumulated as Holy Spirit blessing has distilled all over the earth. But the tragedy of fallen leaders has marred the landscape in drastic and dramatic ways of recent date, and in the blaze of these events a kind of "run-off" has begun. What has surprised me is that I would have supposed the heat of circumstance would have caused everyone involved to "flow" the same direction—along the watercourse cut by the truth and teaching of God's Word. Instead, it seems a watershed moment has occurred, a "continental divide" of sorts, whereby people of adjacency in relationship and mutuality in Christian experience suddenly find themselves moving in opposite directions.

If this were merely a matter of taste or cultural opinion there would be little point in making issue of it. But in the matters of (1) understanding the biblical requirements for spiritual leadership, and of (2) applying those principles in the restoration of leaders who fail their office, we are dealing with truth conclusively set forth in God's Word. There aren't two sides if truth is served; there is only a choice between clarity in direction or confusion of purpose.

In setting forth my concern I write as a pastor. I'm pretty much caught up in concerns which dominate the mind of a shepherd: "How do you lead? What do you feed?" The apostle's words have been ringing in my ears of late:

I charge you therefore before God and the Lord Jesus Christ, who will judge the living and the dead at His appearing and His kingdom: Preach the Word!

Be ready in season and out of season. Convince, rebuke, exhort, with all longsuffering and teaching.

For the time will come when they will not endure sound doctrine, but according to their own desires, because they have itching ears, they will heap up for themselves teachers; and they will turn their ears away from the truth, and be turned aside to fables.

But you be watchful in all things, endure afflictions, do the work of an evangelist, fulfill your ministry.

II Timothy 4:1-5

This is a combined directive and warning. It directs the leader who will listen to beware of the temptation to take the low road to public acceptance. It further warns that there will always be a certain crowd who will clamor for pop-appeal teaching and end up with superficial living. That's the pivotal concern of this small volume.

When one sets out to confront the shallow or the superficial—especially in so brief a message—one is also highly susceptible to either the charge of superficiality (by reason of brevity) or the charge of self-righteousness (for not having sufficiently elaborated the truths of mercy and grace). But I feel neither superior to nor antagonistic toward anyone or any part of the Church. I simply don't want the magnificence of what has been "flowing together unto the goodness of the Lord" (see Jeremiah 31:12) to be either putrified by an indifference to purity or to be confounded by a wandering of any of His flock down the slopes to a sea of deep despair rather than being shepherded toward an ocean of high destiny.

I'm thankful to my friends at Regal Books who encouraged the publication of this message. Though its content is brief I believe the moment is giant and the outflowing of the issue either grand or grotesque, depending upon our personal responses at this watershed season. My prayer is that the "flowing together" that has begun will continue in wisdom and purity—and with power!

In Jesus' life and love,

The Church on the Way
Van Nuys, California

RESTORING FALLEN LEADERS

What do you mean! Don't you think God has for-given them?!!"

"Who gave you the right to judge? We're sick and tired of hearing about it anyway!"

And so one might ask himself, "Why bring up the subject of insisting on *time* as a healing, restorative factor in the recovery of fallen spiritual leaders? Why risk the barrage of questions and criticisms certain to volley forth like a fusillade from a dozen cannons?"

The issue of "*time* for restoration" is a hot one, boiling on the Church's front burner by rea-son of recent events which have forced a focus on such themes as:

- The balance between judgment and mercy,

11

- The requirements of spiritual leadership,
- The relative significance of various sins,
- The submission of leaders to one another,
- The nature of forgiveness and restoration and
- The purpose of the present purging of the Spirit.

I have taken the subject—*the proper requirement of a significant amount of time being applied in a spiritual leader's recovery process*—neither because it's current nor controversial. Rather, I believe its resolution is crucial to the spiritual health of the Body of Christ at this specific time. It's a risky undertaking to say the least. So much misunderstanding abounds. But to neglect addressing the subject involves a greater risk.

> *Not to confront* legalistic demands gives a place to religious notions which forget mercy.
> *Not to challenge* propositions offering cheap grace gives a license to indulgence and irresponsibility.
> *To require too much* of the fallen is to corrupt grace.
> *To require too little* is to cheapen the office of spiritual leadership.

12

To make too much of sexual failure is to appear preoccupied with a pubic theology.

To make too little of it is to surrender to the world's sexual ethics.

To exact various time penalties for different sinning may too easily fall prey to arbitrary judgment.

To expect too little or no time for the restorative process may overlook essential requirements of God's Word.

These are significant issues inherent in the primary issue of *time*, but there is an even larger one.

WHAT'S GOING ON, ANYWAY?

My compelling concern at this juncture, however, is not a self-righteous urge to lash at fallen leaders nor an attempt at omniscience in the face of perplexity. Rather, my motivation is born of a deep concern for all who at any point have participated in the last two decades of a Holy Spirit-fueled revival and renewal.

Great victories of accomplishment in spiritual breakthrough have manifested in many aspects of the interdenominational Body-life of the Church:

If the issue of restoring fallen leaders is not settled in the light of the Word of God and a Holy Spirit-applied ethic; and if the product of a generation of renewal turns out to be a people who cannot balance the biblical demands of judgment and mercy, we are at a tragic end rather than a holy, new beginning.

Multiplied millions have been baptized
in the Spirit;

A new understanding of spiritual gifts
has been gained;

A quickening of the Word in the hearts
of multitudes has inspired faith and service
unto miracle dimensions of ministry;

New centers for training leaders have
blossomed forth; and, quite notably,

A sweeping invasion of the mass media
has taken place through television, radio
and publishing.

But, right now, *the validity and durability of all
the above is on the line.* From my perspective,

if the issue of restoring fallen leaders is not
settled in the light of the Word of God and
a Holy Spirit-applied ethic; and
if the product of a generation of renewal
turns out to be a people who cannot
balance the biblical demands of judgment
and mercy, *we are at a tragic end rather
than a holy, new beginning.*

My conviction is that the Holy Spirit's
will is the latter: *A new beginning.*

The purging, purifying fire of judgment is doing
more than toppling television empires. When any

one is judged we are all wise to recognize that we all—*the whole Body*—are coming under review by the Almighty. The Lord of the Church has stepped into our midst as He did long ago. In Revelation, chapters 2 and 3, He enlisted John's stenographic skills on the Isle of Patmos, dictating His corrective instructions to His Church[1]. The passage might well be summarized as: *"Christ's midcourse navigational adjustments approaching the end of Century I."*

The Captain of Salvation steps to the bridge of the Old Ship Zion, taking firm grip of the helm, commandeering a ship originally intended for victory but now threatened by disaster. In bold strokes with the sword of His mouth, Jesus ferrets out the fruitless, denounces the destructive, condemns the corrupt, commends constancy and promises overcoming triumph to the responsive and the repentant. The result was a Church which moved past the shoals of impending shipwreck and sailed into the next century secure in the lessons of the past and ready for the challenges of the future.

Even now, as we move toward the close of a century which began with a global outpouring of Holy Spirit blessing and which has enjoyed an ever-rising stream of grace bearing the Church forward on a tide of divine power, it's time to be certain we're reading His charts correctly.

All we who comprise the crew of those "enjoying" that tide must now make a sensitive and practical application of God's Word to our present circumstances. If we resort to navigating these stormy times by "seat-of-the-pants" opinion, we're sunk. But if we take our guidance by sounding the depths of truth in the Word of God, we can enter Century XXI on course and under full sail—with the wind of the Spirit billowing us onward in God's will.

A WATERSHED ISSUE

The diversity of opinion on "the issue of time needed for the restoration of a fallen spiritual leader" exposes deep problems. Critically significant to the Church's health is its view of God's Word, the requirements of Christian leadership and the ministering of grace. But it seems somehow these have become muddled and twisted in the present turmoil of dealing with fallen leaders, and beyond that issue itself we have been brought to a watershed point.

Which way will things go?

The nature of the Church—its health, wholeness and holiness—is directly correspondent to our view of the nature of God. How we think about God's character and the manner of His administration of His Kingdom will inevitably determine the

17

formation of our own character and behavior as believers. Straight thinking is crucial; not only about His love, but about how His love *acts* when His children need correction; not only about His mercy, but how He mercifully *judges* when judgment is necessary in His household.

It isn't an exaggeration of the present problem to say that in the last analysis, the Church's view of Jesus' *Lordship* is at stake.

What the Church expects of its spiritual leadership and how we relate to them essentially reflects how Christ Himself is viewed. The Bible says He has "given" each of them as His personal representatives, and as *His* appointed leaders under *His* ultimate headship, they are accountable to *His* terms.

Spiritual leaders have few privileges but many points of responsibility. Basic qualifications for their role are clearly elaborated in the Word. I Timothy 3:1-13, 5:17-15, Titus 1:5-2:8 and I Peter 5:1-11 are foundational in this regard, and mandate character requirements which must be *proven* and *maintained* if a leader is to be found faithful under Christ's Lordship.[2] Any thoughtful study of these expectations reveals a call *not* to a religious rigidity, but to the development of leaders who accept distinct disciplines and who live in a constancy by those standards.

Facing the issues distilling around the trage-

If a surrender to slackness in the requirements of spiritual leadership is conceded now, and if a creeping humanism governs the resolution of this problem, the authority of Christ and His Word will have been supplanted.

dies of fallen spiritual leaders, I see us at a very crucial point. The handling of these issues may well become THE issue of our times. *If a surrender to slackness in the requirements of spiritual leadership is conceded now, and if a creeping humanism governs the resolution of this problem,* the authority of Christ and His Word will have been supplanted. Unless an honest confrontation with *all* the Word of God is made *now,* the result will be nothing less than a reduced view of Christ's Lordship—His rule and His will in His Church.

Why?

Because *He* is the Church's Head. *He* is the One who gives—who appoints His representatives "And He Himself gave some to be apostles, some prophets, some evangelists, and some pastors and teachers" (Ephesians 4:11).

But if these leaders do not own allegiance to *His* standards, ultimately neither will those they lead. Church history verifies this conclusion: inroads of humanistic opinion in the standards governing the selection and sustaining of the Church's leadership *always* eventuate in the corruption of the whole Church. However painful it may be when it comes to ministering the whole truth of the Word when tragic failure befalls a leader, a high view of the requirements for spiritual leadership must be maintained. This will only be done in direct proportion to the degree that a high view of Jesus Himself is maintained.

A balanced look at the Savior shows Him as *both* (1) the Revealer of the Father's heart of love and (2) the Administrator of the Father's hand of justice. The implications of these two facets of Jesus' glorious person are of consummate importance at this time. His gentleness and His judgment—*both* must be held in dynamic tension before the eyes and the understanding of His Church.

We have come too far in a precious movement of near-century-long revival to succumb either to legalism's loveless administration of punishment or to liberalism-in-the-name-of-love's loose handling of a holy assignment. And the determination of exactly *what* is expected of those who lead His flock in Jesus' Name is certainly that: a holy assignment.

To wade into the melee, on the one hand seeking to sustain standards for leadership and, on the other hand seeking to sow mercy and pursue peace, seems an impossible dilemma. That is, unless a point of reference can be agreed upon. Presumably, the Holy Scriptures—the Word of God—is that point for those who read these words. And yet, claiming biblical authority, widely dissonant statements resound everywhere on the matter of restoring fallen leaders.

21

- Arguments for mercy are pled on grounds that, "We're all sinners anyway, and we have no right to judge the fallen" (notwithstanding that I Corinthians 5 and 6, and Matthew 7 require self-judgment by the Body of Christ). [3]
- Pleas for instant return to ministry are made on the grounds, "David wasn't removed as king even though he was immoral and a murderer" (without bothering to study the negative factors that dogged David's life and rule ever after).
- Demands are made for permanent removal from ministry with "no hope of restoration," because "the sacred trust of holy leadership has been violated" (notwithstanding the Savior's proven ability to be able to renew, recreate and restore—II Corinthians 5:17; John 8:1-12—and who if He can beget newness can complete it; Philippians 1:6). [4]
- Insistance on temporary removal and restriction because "a person needs to make some restitution—to pay somehow" (a case of calling for a right action for a wrong reason).

Thus we hear expression of the broad mixture

22

We hear expression of the broad mixture of opinion on the biblical principles of disciplining fallen spiritual leadership, ranging from a laissez-faire indifference about restoration to a pharisaical rush to permanent retirement.

of opinion on the biblical principles of disciplining fallen spiritual leadership, ranging from a laissez-faire indifference about restoration to a pharisaical rush to permanent retirement. But beyond reaction, let us look into the Word on the several questions which constitute the heart of "the issue of time":

(1) The question of the Word's authority,
(2) The question of the preparation or qualification of a spiritual leader,
(3) The question of the tension between "forgiveness" and "the fruits of repentance,"
(4) The question of the meaning of "discipline," and
(5) The possibility of complete restoration of spiritual leaders who have tragically fallen.

AUTHORITY OR SOURCE-BOOK?

The foundational question, "Is God's Word our authority or our occasional Source-book?" is worded so as to distinguish between two attitudes. Ask yourself which governs you:

(1) My opinions formed on the basis of one portion of the Bible must come

under the balancing force of all the
Bible.
(2) My favorite ideas and preferred texts
may selectively hold dominance over
other Scripture passages which
inconvenience my viewpoint.

An example of this second attitude, with reference to how much time should be required for
restoring a fallen spiritual leader, frequent "con-
venient" use being made of Galatians 6:1:

*"Brethren, if a man is overtaken in any
trespass, you who are spiritual restore
such a one in a spirit of gentleness,
considering yourself lest you also be
tempted."*

It's a magnificent verse—but as magnanimous
as it is in its goal of full recovery, it's also demanding in its directives for restoration; more so than a
quick quotation of the verse suggests.

First, an accurate definition of "restore"—its
meaning and tense—dictates a radically different
stance from that assumed by those demanding a
leader's quick return to office. The verb *katartidzo*
(restore) means "to mend, to fit or to thoroughly
equip," and the tense and mood (present impera-
tive) dictate that the action is intended to be sus-

tained in an ongoing, continual way. The clear command as instructed here might appropriately be paraphrased:

"When another person is overtaken in a fault or failure, you who are spiritual people will see to it that you graciously set about the extended task of seeing that person mended and returned to full fitness; doing it in a way that clearly indicates you do not hold yourself as superior to them for their having fallen and all the while remembering your own vulnerability."

The employment of extended time in restoration is specifically dictated by this oft-quoted verse. Rather than the immediate or quick return which glib usage suggests, the text actually requires precisely the opposite. Opinion has nothing to do with it. The Bible simply says it.

I was at a recent gathering of several dozen prominent charismatic leaders, when the leader of the meeting rose and unexpectedly declared: "I believe God is a Restorer, don't you?"

The room chorused a hearty, "Amen!" with my voice chiming in as boldly as any.

Then, the leader called a brother forward—one among us who is deeply beloved, but—who only weeks before had been charged with a gross violation of his duty as a spiritual leader. There-upon, the meeting's leader called us all to join in prayer for the *immediate* "restoration" of the man. It was a bewildering moment.

There was none in the room more anxious than I for the brother's full return to trustworthy minis-try. Like everyone there, I felt no judgment or unforgiveness toward him for his sad failure. But as the prayer was offered, a curious mixture of responses was detectable. The hearty "Amen!" uttered earlier was dissipated now, though a lov-ing supportiveness for a broken brother remained present. The reason for the limited agreement was apparent: A confusion of opinion existed with some as to the meaning of Galatians 6:1, and what it means when it says, "Restore!" "Brethren, if a man is overtaken in any trespass, you who are spiritual restore such a one in a spirit of gentle-ness, considering yourself lest you also be tempted."

To "restore" doesn't mean to return to office or to reinstate in position. According to God's Word, *no* office is actually given by man anyway. All offices in the Body of Christ are ordained by Christ.

"And *He Himself gave* some to be apostles, some prophets, some evangelists, and some pas-tors and teachers" (Ephesians 4:11, emphasis added).

27

What men cannot give in the first place, except under Christ's authority, they are equally unable to restore on other terms than Christ's.

However, men are charged with the responsibility to confirm and place leaders in spiritual office; but only on the terms of the Bible's requirements. The presumption of self-appointment or hasty resumption of spiritual leadership *outside* those requirements is biblically unjustified. What men cannot give in the first place, except under Christ's authority, they are equally unable to restore on other terms than Christ's.

However, what men *can* do is to not only require time, but to give it as well—to the fallen with loving attention and the supporting grace of understanding. This advances the process by which wounded personalities are healed, by which they may be refitted over a period of time that they may once again serve the Body of Christ.

ANOTHER MISUSED TEXT

Another carelessly used Scripture is the misappropriation of Jesus' words concerning "the adulterous look." This has been appealed to where sexual immorality has been the spiritual leader's failure. The usual argument which is attempted to justify the idea that upon confession and repentance the fallen may immediately resume leadership goes something like this:

> "Who among us is guiltless of having 'looked lustfully'? None, of course.

Therefore, since Jesus equated this with
having already committed adultery,
wouldn't *every one* of us need to withdraw
from spiritual leadership? Right! And since
that proposition is ridiculous, isn't it clear
that confession and repentance are
sufficient to provide immediate forgiveness
and the right to continue ongoing
leadership?"

The glaring problem with this half-truth (for
"immediate forgiveness" *is* truly available) is that
it bypasses the crucial distinction between sins "of
the heart" (*potential* sin) and sins "against the
body" (the impact of *actual* sin). In Matthew 5:28,
Jesus charges us with the severity of the soul's
compromise when the eye indulges itself and the
mind entertains lust:

"'But I say to you that whoever looks at a
woman to lust for her has already committed adultery with her in his heart.'"

Jesus insists that *before God,* who looks upon
the heart, sins of the heart *do* need repentance
and cleansing.

This warning *can't* be and *isn't* being mini-
mized.

Jesus' warning amplifies Proverbs 4:23: "Keep
your heart with all diligence, for out of it spring the

issues of life." He focuses on (1) our need for heart purity and (2) the imminent danger of tolerating mental impurity.

But while Jesus shows internal and external sins are equal before God, He didn't declare an equivalency in *heart*-sin and *action*-sin as far as their impact is felt in the arena of human experience. This isn't a rationalization; the Bible actually uses different terminology.

Whereas Jesus warns against *imagined* sinning "in your heart," elsewhere the Word of God describes *actual*, physical immorality as "sinning against your body" (I Corinthians 6:18). The Scriptures also teach that the believer's final accounting before Christ will deal with those things he has done *physically*: "For we must all appear before the judgment seat of Christ, that each one may receive the things done in the body, according to what he has done, whether good or bad" (II Corinthians 5:10). This isn't to minimize sinful attitudes. Jesus' words *are* intended to nip the nub of budding lust, but they *aren't* intended to equalize the internal erosion by thoughts of sin with the external destructiveness of sin's actions.

The simple fact that no one ever became pregnant or contracted venereal disease for having "sinned in his heart" shows the impact and influence of *committed* sin exceeds that of imagined sin. Even so our sincere pursuit of pleasing God

31

does require us to deal with lust at the heart-level—purifying our minds and securing our souls against the carnally corrupt.

There is a vast difference in what happens when a leader *thinks* impurely and when he *acts* that way. When he sins, a destructive chain reaction of pain occurs. Sin of whatever nature—sexual, financial, doctrinal, brutal, relational—brings a blow "against the body."

1. The leader who submits to temptation and actually sins compromises his office. He sins against the "Body" he serves.
2. The emotional impact and spiritual injury to his marriage can hardly be measured. He sins against the "body" of the "one flesh" union between him and his spouse.
3. The onlooking world mocks the Church, not only for failure but for inconsistent discipline. The *whole* "Body" is cheapened in the eyes of a laughing world.

This trickle-down effect only happens when sin occurs "against the body." The misuse of Matthew 5:28 as a neutralizer of proper time restrictions crumbles under the evidence of the Word and

A fallen leader's fall may have come as the result of unworthy thoughts, but the problem is because his failure penetrated the field of action.

reason. Both deny such confusion.

A fallen leader's fall may have come as the result of unworthy thoughts, but the problem is because his failure penetrated the field of action. Not only has the leader's *own* person and home been scarred, but far more drastically, that segment of *the* "Body" which he leads has been injured. A time for the healing process for him, his marriage and his sheep must be set in motion.

The issue in this misuse of Galatians 6:1 and Matthew 5:28 transcends their misinterpretation in the problem of fallen leaders. Such a selective, convenience-oriented approach to Scripture warns us of an impending mutiny against the Word's authority over our lives. It's a sobering fact which underscores the truth that recklessness on this "issue of time" is closer than we may realize to being THE issue of our times.

"GROWN" OR "CLAIMED"

Second, it takes time to restore a fallen spiritual leader because it took time to make him one. The position of spiritual leadership is *not one* that is "claimed"—that is, simply assumed or even humanly assigned, it is one into which a person matures.

In the earlier mentioned passages from the Epistles, the Holy Spirit explicitly mandates cer-

34

tain qualifications, all of which can only be arrived at with *time*. Thus, I Timothy 3:10, in referring to the identifying of spiritual leadership, says, "Let them be first proved"; that is, besides the time required to cultivate the character traits required, they are to be "tested" (proved).

Dokimadzo (proved) is the Greek word used to describe a tried-in-the-fire order of testing, and refers to that which is refined and tempered through experience. So when the tests of life reveal "cracks" in the character of a leader and produce scandalous conduct, an overnight return to duty violates the original principles of his appointment.

Haste in appointment is specifically prohibited. That's why, two chapters later, Paul further instructs Timothy, "Do not lay hands on anyone hastily" (I Timothy 5:22).

New Testament leaders are *grown*—matured and seasoned over time, and verified in character and conduct *before* hands are laid upon them, confirming the grace and call of God on their lives.

But what happens when a leader so proven and dedicated to ministry falls?

FORGIVENESS AND FRUITFULNESS

The failure of a spiritual leader is a staggeringly painful event in the life of everyone affected by that person. Some argue that God lets leaders fall to break down the idolatry in the hearts of those who so admiringly follow the leader. I disagree completely.

While isolated cases of idolizing of leadership may inevitably be present in the Body of Christ, by and large the admiration, the emulation and the appreciation accorded leaders is neither unspiritual nor improper. God intends leaders to "grow" into that kind of respectability and trustworthiness.

Shepherds of God's flock are never intended to feign or fake those qualities for the purpose of securing trust, but neither are the sheep out of order for looking up to and following the example of a good shepherd. Thus, when a shepherd fails—not when mere human idiosyncrasy or imperfection manifests itself, but when scandalous sin occurs—the flock is unsettled and shaken.

It is an unfortunate trait of human nature that when a devoted spiritual leader falls, the people he or she leads are so emotionally impacted and bereft of the security they have felt in their spiritual relationship to that person, that rarely are their emotions controlled. While a few may express anger, the disposition of most of the sheep, bruised in spirit by the fall of their shepherd, is to seize on the greatest point of support we all have—the *grace* of God.

That grace, which *always* brings instant and

36

complete forgiveness wherever full-hearted and genuine repentance is present, becomes their overarching point of appeal, but its application is pressed beyond forgiveness to reinstatement. All too quickly, and for understandable yet unjustified emotional reasons, their voices lift an appeal for an instant settlement of the problem—a quick relief for their pain.

Their cries gush forth:

> "We're all sinners saved by grace: he/ she is just another one of us. We love him/ her. Jesus has forgiven him/her. We do too."

> "Who are we to judge? God's grace is immediate and his/her repentance is so clearly evident. So he/she failed—But we will restore him/her now, like the Bible says."

> "The gifts and calling of God don't change—the Bible says so. He/she is our leader, and we accept him/her back, no matter what has happened—it's past."

It all sounds so biblical, so spiritual and so lovingly gracious. And insofar as God's *forgiveness* of the leader is concerned, it is all so completely true. But forgiveness and fruitfulness are two different things.

Forgiveness is instantaneous, but the fruits of repentance take time to grow. The restoration of the scorched fruitage of years of ministry and the repair of the "cracks" in the character which sinning has exposed cannot be restored in a moment's burst of gracious intent or holy passion.

It is characteristic of most recommendations for quick restoration that too casual an attitude exists concerning the *time* which was involved in leading to the sin, or the time involved in *continuing* the sinful walk *to* which the leader submitted. When grace forgives and then God's Word summons to time for healing and full recovery of the person, it is time to remember: What takes time to break takes time to mend.

Sin isn't the fruit of a moment; neither is restoration.

Although the basic worth of the individual's experience and wisdom has not been completely lost, and though he may well be "sadder but wiser" for having failed, the fallen leader must reestablish a life-style verifying trustworthiness again. Time *must* be required to reestablish scriptural values in his conduct.

The fruitage of:

(1) orderly personal church and family relationships,

Although the basic worth of the individual's experience and wisdom has not been completely lost, and though he may well be "sadder but wiser" for having failed, the fallen leader must reestablish a life-style verifying trustworthiness again.

(2) proper personal life and money management and

(3) reliability in living what is taught; all this must be given *time* to be verified.

It is outright dishonesty with the psychological facts of the human personality to suppose an overnight or quick-fix healing in relationships or trust is as immediate as the blessing of God's instant forgiveness.

DISCIPLINE OR PUNISHMENT?

It's a sad fact that many believers see the disciplining of a spiritual leader as an effort on man's part to punish, embarrass or retaliate. If such unworthy motives have ever been present, they were as unbiblical as the leader's tragic fall. But the requirement of time for restoration is not a punishment—it is an opportunity for another side of "grace" to be shown.

Failure takes various forms—the mishandling of monies, deception in teaching the Word, immorality in relationships, brutality in conduct, mounting of ecclesiastical warfare, etc. Whenever one or more of these failures befall a spiritual leader, a certain wisdom must be applied. It is needful that (1) repentance be humbly manifest and that (2) submission to the restoration process be allowed. The leader needs to declare *both* before those he

40

leads and those who are his peers or leaders in ministry.

That his repentance include his commitment to time for his restoration cannot be mandated apart from his own will to do so. But honesty requires an acknowledgment of the realities of our human nature; time is needed to *heal* and time is needed to restore trust.

For example, where sexual failure has occurred and a marriage been violated the sinning leader is not the sole victim of his sin. Besides the other party, a spouse has also been deeply wounded, a marriage has been sorely violated and a life-long trust has been ripped to the core.

Emotions may appear controlled in public, and even in private; but it is foolish to overlook the fact that they've been shredded. Not only does the couple's marriage need to have time sheltered from the rigors of leadership duties in order to service the repair of their union, but the foundations of that leader's qualifications need repair as well.

Among the foundational requirements for married spiritual leaders is that they "be faithful in all things . . . be the husbands of one wife, ruling [leading] their children and their own houses well" (I Timothy 3:10-12). The events occasioning the sad failure have raised questions which can only be satisfied by allowing a period of time before renewing their privilege to leadership:

(1) Faithfulness has been violated—they *weren't* "faithful in all things";

(2) A second "spouse" invaded the relationship—there *was* more than "one wife";

(3) The children's trust and the home's order have both been broken—the home *wasn't* "ruled well."

These are not matters that can be reverified in a moment—or in a few weeks.

Yes, forgiveness on everyone's part, including God's, may be instant but the fruit of proven character takes time to be regrown.

BUT WE NEED THEM!

Tearful and sometime indignant cries are raised when the biblical truth of insistence upon a time of restoration is pressed. Hollow arguments rise: "What about King David? He continued to rule after his failure."

But no one goes on to elaborate

(1) that the infant died,

(2) that David testifies to at least a year of internal agony,

(3) that his household was a shambles from that day forward and

It is a sorry dismissal of the Bible's teaching when anyone proposes an evidence of the truth that violation *by* spiritual leadership means disqualification *from* spiritual leadership.

(4) that the glory years of his leadership never reappeared.

Another cries, "But what of the souls that might be lost if we deprive them of ministry!" Few bother to be honest with the fact that God needs *none* of us, though He lovingly welcomes *all* of us who will allow Him to use us on His terms.

The Apostle Paul warned of the price of a spiritual leader's removal from office through failure. "But I discipline my body and bring it into subjection, lest, when I have preached to others, I myself should become disqualified" (I Corinthians 9:27). Every leader has been forewarned by that trumpet call to vigilance sounded in the Word of God.

Failure disqualifies, and requalification takes *time*. It is a sorry dismissal of the Bible's teaching when anyone proposes an evidence of the truth that violation *by* spiritual leadership means disqualification *from* spiritual leadership.

We must seriously face the issue of time the way God's Word requires. Regretfully, it is too late to cry, "We need them!" after the tragedy of disqualification has occurred. The biblical terms of spiritual leadership mandate that the whole Body prioritize the requirements for each leader, and *not* sacrifice them on a self-serving altar of exigency.

As fruitful as any ministry may have been, let

us be reminded that God is never dependent upon any particular human being to accomplish His will. The *Body* of Christ is His channel of ministry, and any member He uses is dispensable. It is a delusion of sincere sheep to suppose any shepherd, however gifted or able, is anything more than a privileged and anointed servant of the Most High.

Let us be done with shallow notions that the absence of a dear leader who succumbs to his/her carnal weakness or pride, shall frustrate the consummate purposes of God through the Church His Son died to redeem. Any person may miss their place or miss their reward, but God's high purposes shall not be overthrown: He has the entirety of the Body of His Son to flow His Holy Spirit through to a needy world.

IS RESTORATION POSSIBLE?

Just as some would too readily return a fallen spiritual leader to ministry, there are other sincere believers who would say such failure disqualifies him from *ever* returning to leadership.

What does the Bible say?

First, let us admit it is far easier to administrate a prohibition than to minister a restoration. Yet, there is no biblical justification for rejecting the proposition that redemption and restoration might recover fruit lost in the greatest tragedy.

"I will restore to you the years that the swarming locust has eaten," Joel prophesies (Joel 2:25). His movement through the list of insects which ransacked and stripped the fields bare, and then his holding forth the promise of recovered fruitfulness by the restoring grace of God, are words which heralded the age of the Holy Spirit.

We live in that age today.

And it is precisely that we *do*—that we *are* living in a time when the Holy Spirit is moving so mightily—that *both* the discipline of time and the *promise* it holds must be seen for what they are: to instruct with wisdom and to inspire with hope. To hold forth a forgiving grace in the name of Jesus is the glad tidings we have been commissioned to bring: instant reconciliation with God, new birth in Christ, promised blessing and eternal life forever.

But there is no instant cultivation of character.

People still need to grow in grace and in the knowledge of our Lord Jesus Christ. "Giving all diligence, add to your faith virtue, to virtue knowledge, to knowledge self-control, to self-control perseverance, to perseverance godliness, to godliness brotherly kindness, and to brotherly kindness love" (II Peter 1:5-7).

That is the believer's call to discipleship—to the disciplines of a full-hearted follower of Jesus. And thus, when a leader falls, *if* he will submit himself to spiritual discipline under the care of other

When a leader falls, *if* he will submit himself to spiritual discipline under the care of other elders who will love, serve and assist his restoration through their care and kindness, discipline will be realized.

elders who will love, serve and assist his restoration through their care and kindness, discipline will be realized.

"The discipline of a fallen leader" is not a punishment by others. It is a voluntarily accepted role of one who believes the full teaching of the Word about three things: God's mercy in forgiveness, God's summons to restoration and the obligation of every spiritual leader to accept the counsel of other leaders in the spirit of submission.

That's what "the discipline of time" is about: healing and mending, not punishment. And the one who accepts that discipline becomes a disciple again, at a fresh point of beginning—forgiven and cleansed, and ready for the process of recovery.

Let us never doubt that by God's Holy Spirit and in accordance with His Word, such a recovery can be complete.

HOW MUCH TIME?

At the bottom line, the practical question of "calendaring restoration" comes under inquiry. How long is to be required? How much time is needed? Who is to say, set and monitor the time? What does the Bible say about the matter?

Some conclude that the Bible *has* spoken on the subject. They cite David's adultery, Jonah's running and Peter's denial as biblical precedents arguing for an unbroken continuance of leadership, if not a short time of recompense for restoration. But in the light of the larger issues already elaborated, in which the requirements of character and conduct have been shown to be foundational to spiritual leadership, these episodes present a rather weak case.

We have already discussed the general overlooking of the *full* details of David's story, but what about Jonah's flight from God's commission to Nineveh, and Peter's denial? Without appearing to whitewash either for their lack of courage, neither Peter nor Jonah were financially dishonest, immoral, guilty of teaching false doctrine or puffed up with arrogant pride. Neither was guilty of scandal. Neither failed a body of believers in the sense that today's Church leader may impact the group he serves.

But, both Peter and Jonah *were* guilty of *fear*—committing sin of temporary weakness and failure more than of a calculated process of surrender to serving as part of a permanent plan. Their failures were more of cowardliness than of corruption.

If Jonah and Peter demonstrate anything about failure in spiritual leadership, they seem to show the difference between failing the Lord at a personal level and failing a body of believers as their leaders; of stumbling for a moment as opposed to

49

Spiritual leaders usually fall as the result of having been deceived by Satan and having disobeyed the Holy Spirit's warnings.

pursuing a pattern of *surrender* to ongoing temptation. They both failed the Lord but neither violated a body of believers. Whatever may be attempted at making a case for a quick reentry to ministry after a leader's severe fall, these cases from the Bible can only be seized upon at the expense of dishonesty with the issue of time as it relates to renewing healing, restoring relationship and reestablishing trustworthiness.

In the absence of an explicit biblical directive as to the amount of time necessary for restoration, what guidelines do we have? I think there are three.

First, beware of any preoccupation with too quick a return. Such a disposition by the fallen one probably signals a resident presumption or shallow repentance, and such a disposition by those sincerely wanting to affirm the fallen usually indicates an immature perspective on the nature and requirements of spiritual leadership.

Second, beware of overlooking the depth of the fallen's injury. One of the most human responses in the world is to attempt a sudden scrambling to your feet when you have been embarrassed by having slipped or fallen. Spiritual leaders usually fall as the result of both, having been deceived by Satan and having disobeyed the Holy Spirit's warnings.

Now, as the victims of deception and disobedience, deep, deep wounds exist in the human psyche. Aside from the biblical propriety of giving time

(1) to renew evidence of a "whole" character and

(2) to renew personal relationships which have been transgressed,

(3) we need to verify that deep pain is not masked or bandaged with superficial or platitudinous counsel.

An accident victim may be treated immediately in the emergency ward and his life spared. But regaining the use of damaged limbs requires patience and therapy.

Third, beware of unilateral or "pop" methods of reinstatement. Self-announcement is not the biblical pathway to leadership; neither is demagoguery.

There is a "pop" way of "playing to the crowd" of one's sympathizers or supporters, and by this ploy a leader can manipulate his supporters and seek to justify his premature, unscriptural return to ministry on the grounds of the general acceptance or insistence of his followers. The problem with such a style is that it contains nothing of the spirit of submission which is at the foundation of all true spiritual authority.

Irrespective of what terminology one employs or which form of church government he acknowledges, the Bible shows *all* ministry is to be confirmed by "a presbytery"; that is, a group of elders (1) who meet the requirements of character and conduct qualifications and (2) who are committed to lay hands on and endorse only those who do also.

It would be pretentious for any group or denomination to suppose they had mastered the issue of "how much time" restoration requires; but it would be equally foolish and presumptuous for any individual to resist the accumulated wisdom of years reflected in the decision-making of such groups and to arrogantly suppose his own personal system to be superior.

It is not without reason that so many groups recommend or require from one to even four or five years for the recovery of fallen leaders. More and more are accepting a greater responsibility for caring for their fallen: providing transitional financial assistance, expense for counseling, personal support groups and guidance toward recovery. The strength of this development in the larger Body of Christ is not only in the Christlike care it shows, but in the biblical value being served: Time for restoration—time that is required, but also time that is filled with redemptive action.

A RISK; A HOPE

In writing these pages, I have realized that my

The Lordship of Jesus Christ is not at stake in the ultimate order of things, but our will to accept His Lordly rule in the governing of His Church is very much in question at the present.

doing so was at a very real personal risk of being misunderstood. One becomes very vulnerable to being thought self-righteous, prudish, small-minded, merciless or judgmental. Further, events of recent months create a climate that the article may be suspected as some type of backhanded slap at renowned brethren who have fallen. But I have determined to accept these risks in the light of what, to my view, is a far greater issue: the pivotal time at which the Body of Christ presently lives.

As I observed at the onset, a near-century of the moving of God's Spirit is coming under review as to its relative substance and as to its biblical foundation. The Lordship of Jesus Christ is not at stake in the ultimate order of things, but our will to accept His Lordly rule in the governing of His Church is very much in question at the present.

If the qualifications of those leaders representing His leadership overall are allowed to be goaded by humanistic reasoning rather than guided by divine revelation, the destiny of those influenced by such outright neglect of Scripture is doomed to confusion and ultimately to defeat.

My persuasion is that great hope is before us; that the concluding years of this millennium and the opening of the next are scheduled by the Holy Spirit to be unprecedented in blessing. By the same token, the evidence of Scripture is that the same season of time shall involve our confrontation with increasingly hostile works of hell.

Thus, with the highest promise and the greatest warfare before us, the ranks of Christ's army must now—more than ever—heed the guidelines of God's Word. Disciplined disciples who grow to lead by following in Christ's likeness and spirit will lead the Church to triumph.

It is the time to triumph.

It's worth taking time to be certain we do.

NOTES

Note 1

REVELATION 2:1-29

The Loveless Church

"To the angel of the church of Ephesus write,

'These things says He who holds the seven stars in His right hand, who walks in the midst of the seven golden lampstands:

"I know your works, your labor, your patience, and that you cannot bear those who are evil. And you have tested those who say they are apostles and are not, and have found them liars;

"and you have persevered and have patience, and have labored for My name's sake and have not become weary.

"Nevertheless I have *this* against you, that you have left your first love.

"Remember therefore from where you have fallen; repent and do the first works, or else I will come to you quickly and remove your lampstand from its place—unless you repent.

"But this you have, that you hate the deeds of the Nicolaitans, which I also hate.

"He who has an ear, let him hear what the Spirit says to the churches. To him who overcomes I will give to eat from the tree of life, which is in the midst of the Paradise of God.'"

The Persecuted Church

"And to the angel of the church in Smyrna write,

'These things says the First and the Last, who was dead, and came to life:

"I know your works, tribulation, and poverty (but you are rich); and I *know* the blasphemy of those who say they are Jews and are not, but *are* a synagogue of Satan.

"Do not fear any of those things which you are about to suffer. Indeed, the devil is about to throw *some* of you into prison, that you may be tested, and you will have tribulation ten days. Be faithful until death, and I will give you the crown of life.

"He who has an ear, let him hear what the Spirit says to the churches. He who overcomes shall not be hurt by the second death.'"

The Compromising Church

"And to the angel of the church in Pergamos write,

'These things says He who has the sharp two-edged sword:

"I know your works, and where you dwell, where Satan's throne *is*. And you hold fast to My name, and did not deny My faith even in the days in which Antipas *was* My faithful martyr, who was killed among you, where Satan dwells.

"But I have a few things against you, because you have there those who hold the doctrine of Balaam, who taught Balak to put a stumbling block before the children of Israel, to eat things sacrificed to idols, and to commit sexual immorality.

"Thus you also have those who hold the doctrine of the Nicolaitans, which thing I hate.

'Repent, or else I will come to you quickly and will fight against them with the sword of My mouth.

"He who has an ear, let him hear what the Spirit says to the churches. To him who overcomes I will give some of the hidden manna to eat. And I will give him a white stone, and on the stone a new name written which no one knows except him who receives *it.*"'

The Corrupt Church
"And to the angel of the church in Thyatira write,

'These things says the Son of God, who has eyes like a flame of fire, and His feet like fine brass:

"I know your works, love, service, faith, and your patience; and *as* for your works, the last *are* more than the first.

"Nevertheless I have a few things against you, because you allow that woman Jezebel, who calls herself a prophetess, to teach and beguile My servants to commit sexual immorality and to eat things sacrificed to idols.

"And I gave her time to repent of her sexual immorality, and she did not repent.

"Indeed I will cast her into a sickbed, and those who commit adultery with her into great tribulation, unless they repent of their deeds.

"And I will kill her children with death. And all the churches shall know that I am He who searches the minds and hearts. And I will give to each one of you according to your works.

"But to you I say, and to the rest in Thyatira, as many as do not have this doctrine, and who have not known the depths of Satan, as they call *them,* I will put on you no other burden.

"But hold fast what you have till I come.

"And he who overcomes, and keeps My works until the end, to him I will give power over the nations—

> *'He shall rule them*
> *with a rod of iron;*
> *As the potter's vessels*
> *shall be broken to pieces'*—

as I also have received from My Father;

"and I will give him the morning star.

"He who has an ear, let him hear what the Spirit says to the churches.'"

REVELATION 3:1-22

The Dead Church

"And to the angel of the church in Sardis write,

'These things says He who has the seven Spirits of God and the seven stars: "I know your works, that you have a name that you are alive, but you are dead.

"Be watchful, and strengthen the things which remain, that are ready to die, for I have not found your works perfect before God.

"Remember therefore how you have received and heard; hold fast and repent. Therefore if you will not watch, I will come upon you as a thief, and you will not know what hour I will come upon you.

"You have a few names even in Sardis who have not defiled their garments; and they shall walk with Me in white, for they are worthy.

"He who overcomes shall be clothed in white

garments, and I will not blot out his name from the Book of Life; but I will confess his name before My Father and before His angels.

"He who has an ear, let him hear what the Spirit says to the churches.'"

The Faithful Church

"And to the angel of the church in Philadelphia write,

'These things says He who is holy, He who is true, *He who has the key of David, He who opens and no one shuts, and shuts and no one opens*':

"I know your works. See, I have set before you an open door, and no one can shut it; for you have a little strength, have kept My word, and have not denied My name.

"Indeed I will make *those* of the synagogue of Satan, who say they are Jews and are not, but lie—indeed I will make them come and worship before your feet, and to know that I have loved you.

"Because you have kept My command to persevere, I also will keep you from the hour of trial which shall come upon the whole world, to test those who dwell on the earth.

"Behold, I come quickly! Hold fast what you have, that no one may take your crown.

"He who overcomes, I will make him a pillar in the temple of My God, and he shall go out no more. And I will write on him the name of My God and the name of the city of My God, the New Jerusalem, which comes down out of heaven from My God. And *I will write on him* My new name.

"He who has an ear, let him hear what the Spirit says to the churches."

The Lukewarm Church

"And to the angel of the church of the Laodiceans write,

'These things says the Amen, the Faithful and True Witness, the Beginning of the creation of God:

"I know your works, that you are neither cold nor hot. I could wish you were cold or hot.

"So then, because you are lukewarm, and neither cold nor hot, I will spew you out of My mouth.

"Because you say, 'I am rich, have become wealthy, and have need of nothing'—and do not know that you are wretched, miserable, poor, blind, and naked—

"I counsel you to buy from Me gold refined in the fire, that you may be rich; and white garments, that you may be clothed, *that* the shame of your nakedness may not be revealed; and anoint your eyes with eye salve, that you may see.

"As many as I love, I rebuke and chasten. Therefore be zealous and repent.

"Behold, I stand at the door and knock. If anyone hears My voice and opens the door, I will come in to him and dine with him, and he with Me.

"To him who overcomes I will grant to sit with Me on My throne, as I also overcame and sat down with My Father on His throne.

"He who has an ear, let him hear what the Spirit says to the churches." ' "

Note 2

I TIMOTHY 3:1-13

Qualifications of Overseers

This *is* a faithful saying: If a man desires the position of a bishop, he desires a good work.

A bishop then must be blameless, the husband of one wife, temperate, sober-minded, of good behavior, hospitable, able to teach;

not given to wine, not violent, not greedy for money, but gentle, not quarrelsome, not covetous;

one who rules his own house well, having *his* children in submission with all reverence

(for if a man does not know how to rule his own house, how will he take care of the church of God?);

not a novice, lest being puffed up with pride he fall into the *same* condemnation as the devil.

Moreover he must have a good testimony

among those who are outside, lest he fall into reproach and the snare of the devil.

Qualifications of Deacons

Likewise deacons *must be* reverent, not double-tongued, not given to much wine, not greedy for money,

holding the mystery of the faith with a pure conscience.

But let these also first be proved; then let them serve as deacons, being *found* blameless.

Likewise *their* wives *must be* reverent, not slanderers, temperate, faithful in all things.

Let deacons be the husbands of one wife, ruling *their* children and their own houses well.

For those who have served well as deacons obtain for themselves a good standing and great boldness in the faith which is in Christ Jesus.

I TIMOTHY 5:17-25

Honor the Elders

Let the elders who rule well be counted worthy of double honor, especially those who labor in the word and doctrine.

For the Scripture says, *"You shall not muzzle an ox while it treads out the grain,"* and, "The laborer *is* worthy of his wages."

Do not receive an accusation against an elder

except from two or three witnesses.

Those who are sinning rebuke in the presence of all, that the rest also may fear.

I charge *you* before God and the Lord Jesus Christ and the elect angels that you observe these things without prejudice, doing nothing with partiality.

Do not lay hands on anyone hastily, nor share in other people's sins; keep yourself pure.

No longer drink only water, but use a little wine for your stomach's sake and your frequent infirmities.

Some men's sins are clearly evident, preceding *them* to judgment, but those of some *men* follow later.

Likewise, the good works *of some* are clearly evident, and those that are otherwise cannot be hidden.

TITUS 1:5–2:8

Qualified Elders

For this reason I left you in Crete, that you should set in order the things that are lacking, and appoint elders in every city as I commanded you—

if a man is blameless, the husband of one wife, having faithful children not accused of dissipation or insubordination.

For a bishop must be blameless, as a steward of God, not self-willed, not quick-tempered, not given to wine, not violent, not greedy for money,

but hospitable, a lover of what is good, sober-minded, just, holy, self-controlled,

holding fast the faithful word as he has been taught, that he may be able, by sound doctrine, both to exhort and convict those who contradict.

The Elders' Task

For there are many insubordinate, both idle talkers and deceivers, especially those of the circumcision,

whose mouths must be stopped, who subvert whole households, teaching things which they ought not, for the sake of dishonest gain.

One of them, a prophet of their own, said, "Cretans *are* always liars, evil beasts, lazy gluttons."

This testimony is true. Therefore rebuke them sharply, that they may be sound in the faith,

not giving heed to Jewish fables and commandments of men who turn from the truth.

To the pure all things are pure, but to those who are defiled and unbelieving nothing is pure; but even their mind and conscience are defiled.

They profess to know God, but in works they deny Him, being abominable, disobedient, and disqualified for every good work.

TITUS 2:1-8

Qualities of a Sound Church

But as for you, speak the things which are proper for sound doctrine:

that the older men be sober, reverent, temperate, sound in faith, in love, in patience;

the older women likewise, that they be reverent in behavior, not slanderers, not given to much wine, teachers of good things—

that they admonish the young women to love their husbands, to love their children,

to be discreet, chaste, homemakers, good, obedient to their own husbands, that the word of God may not be blasphemed.

Likewise exhort the young men to be sober-minded,

in all things showing yourself *to be* a pattern of good works; in doctrine *showing* integrity, reverence, incorruptibility,

sound speech that cannot be condemned, that one who is an opponent may be ashamed, having nothing evil to say of you.

I PETER 5:1-11

Shepherd the Flock

The elders who are among you I exhort, I who

am a fellow elder and a witness of the sufferings of Christ, and also a partaker of the glory that will be revealed:

Shepherd the flock of God which is among you, serving as overseers, not by constraint but willingly, not for dishonest gain but eagerly;

nor as being lords over those entrusted to you, but being examples to the flock;

and when the Chief Shepherd appears, you will receive the crown of glory that does not fade away.

Submit to God, Resist the Devil

Likewise you younger people, submit yourselves to *your* elders. Yes, all of *you* be submissive to one another, and be clothed with humility, for *"God resists the proud, But gives grace to the humble."*

Therefore humble yourselves under the mighty hand of God, that He may exalt you in due time,

casting all your care upon Him, for He cares for you.

Be sober, be vigilant; because your adversary the devil walks about like a roaring lion, seeking whom he may devour.

Resist him, steadfast in the faith, knowing that the same sufferings are experienced by your brotherhood in the world.

But may the God of all grace, who called us to His eternal glory by Christ Jesus, after you have suffered a while, perfect, establish, strengthen, and settle *you*.

To Him *be* the glory and the dominion forever and ever. Amen.

Note 3

I CORINTHIANS 5:1-13

Immorality Defiles the Church

It is actually reported *that there is* sexual immorality among you, and such sexual immorality as is not even named among the Gentiles—that a man has his father's wife!

And you are puffed up, and have not rather mourned, that he who has done this deed might be taken away from among you.

For I indeed, as absent in body but present in spirit, have already judged, as though I were present, *concerning* him who has so done this deed.

In the name of our Lord Jesus Christ, when you are gathered together, along with my spirit, with the power of our Lord Jesus Christ,

deliver such a one to Satan for the destruction of the flesh, that his spirit may be saved in the day of the Lord Jesus.

Your glorying *is* not good. Do you not know that a little leaven leavens the whole lump?

Therefore purge out the old leaven, that you may be a new lump, since you truly are unleavened. For indeed Christ, our Passover, was sacrificed for us.

Therefore let us keep the feast, not with old leaven, nor with the leaven of malice and wickedness, but with the unleavened *bread* of sincerity and truth.

Immorality Must Be Judged

I write to you in my epistle not to keep company with sexually immoral people.

Yet *I* certainly *did* not *mean* with the sexually immoral people of this world, or with the covetous, or extortioners, or idolaters, since then you would need to go out of the world.

But now I have written to you not to keep company with anyone named a brother, who is a fornicator, or covetous, or an idolater, or a reviler, or a drunkard, or an extortioner—not even to eat with such a person.

For what *have* I *to do* with judging those also who are outside? Do you not judge those who are inside?

But those who are outside God judges. Therefore *"put away from yourselves that wicked person."*

71

I CORINTHIANS 6:1-20

Do Not Sue the Brethren

Dare any of you, having a matter against another, go to law before the unrighteous, and not before the saints?

Do you not know that the saints will judge the world? And if the world will be judged by you, are you unworthy to judge the smallest matters?

Do you not know that we shall judge angels? How much more, things that pertain to this life?

If then you have judgments concerning things pertaining to this life, do you appoint those who are least esteemed by the church to judge?

I say this to your shame. Is it so, that there is not a wise man among you, not even one, who will be able to judge between his brethren?

But brother goes to law against brother, and that before unbelievers!

Now therefore, it is already an utter failure for you that you go to law against one another. Why do you not rather accept wrong? Why do you not rather *let yourselves* be defrauded?

No, you yourselves do wrong and defraud, and *you do* these things *to your* brethren!

Do you not know that the unrighteous will not inherit the kingdom of God? Do not be deceived. Neither fornicators, nor idolaters, nor adulterers, nor homosexuals, nor sodomites, nor thieves, nor covetous, nor drunkards, nor revilers, nor extortioners will inherit the kingdom of God.

And such were some of you. But you were washed, but you were sanctified, but you were justified in the name of the Lord Jesus and by the Spirit of our God.

Glorify God in Body and Spirit

All things are lawful for me, but all things are not helpful. All things are lawful for me, but I will not be brought under the power of any.

Foods for the stomach and the stomach for foods, but God will destroy both it and them. Now the body *is* not for sexual immorality but for the Lord, and the Lord for the body.

And God both raised up the Lord and will also raise us up by His power.

Do you not know that your bodies are members of Christ? Shall I then take the members of Christ and make *them* members of a harlot? Certainly not!

Or do you not know that he who is joined to a harlot is one body *with her?* For *"The two,"* He says, *"shall become one flesh."*

But he who is joined to the Lord is one spirit *with Him.*

Flee sexual immorality. Every sin that a man

73

does is outside the body, but he who commits sexual immorality sins against his own body.

Or do you not know that your body is the temple of the Holy Spirit *who is* in you, whom you have from God, and you are not your own?

For you were bought at a price; therefore glorify God in your body and in your spirit, which are God's.

MATTHEW 7: 1-29

Do Not Judge

"Judge not, that you be not judged.

"For with what judgment you judge, you will be judged; and with the *same* measure you use, it will be measured back to you.

"And why do you look at the speck in your brother's eye, but do not consider the plank in your own eye?

"Or how can you say to your brother, 'Let me remove the speck out of your eye'; and look, a plank *is* in your own eye?

"Hypocrite! First remove the plank from your own eye, and then you will see clearly to remove the speck out of your brother's eye.

"Do not give what is holy to the dogs; nor cast your pearls before swine, lest they trample them under their feet, and turn and tear you in pieces.

Keep Asking, Seeking, Knocking

"Ask, and it will be given to you; seek and you will find; knock, and it will be opened to you.

"For everyone who asks receives, and he who seeks finds, and to him who knocks it will be opened.

"Or what man is there among you who, if his son asks for bread, will give him a stone?

"Or if he asks for a fish, will he give him a serpent?

"If you then, being evil, know how to give good gifts to your children, how much more will your Father who is in heaven give good things to those who ask Him!

"Therefore, whatever you want men to do to you, do also to them, for this is the Law and the Prophets.

The Narrow Way

"Enter by the narrow gate; for wide *is* the gate and broad *is* the way that leads to destruction, and there are many who go in by it.

"Because narrow *is* the gate and difficult *is* the way which leads to life, and there are few who find it.

You Will Know Them by Their Fruits

"Beware of false prophets, who come to you in sheep's clothing, but inwardly they are ravenous wolves.

"You will know them by their fruits. Do men gather grapes from thornbushes or figs from thistles?

"Even so, every good tree bears good fruit, but a bad tree bears bad fruit.

"A good tree cannot bear bad fruit, nor *can* a bad tree bear good fruit.

"Every tree that does not bear good fruit is cut down and thrown into the fire.

"Therefore by their fruits you will know them.

I Never Knew You

"Not everyone who says to Me, 'Lord, Lord,' shall enter the kingdom of heaven, but he who does the will of My Father in heaven.

"Many will say to Me in that day, 'Lord, Lord, have we not prophesied in Your name, cast out demons in Your name, and done many wonders in Your name?'

"And then I will declare to them, 'I never knew you; depart from Me, you who practice lawlessness!'

Build on the Rock

"Therefore whoever hears these sayings of Mine, and does them, I will liken him to a wise man who built his house on the rock:

"and the rain descended, the floods came, and

76

the winds blew and beat on that house; and it did not fall, for it was founded on the rock.

"Now everyone who hears these sayings of Mine, and does not do them, will be like a foolish man who built his house on the sand:

"and the rain descended, the floods came, and the winds blew and beat on that house; and it fell. And great was its fall."

And so it was, when Jesus had ended these sayings, that the people were astonished at His teaching,

for He taught them as one having authority, and not as the scribes.

Note 4

II CORINTHIANS 5:17

Therefore, if anyone *is* in Christ, *he is* a new creation; old things have passed away; behold, all things have become new.

JOHN 8:1-12

An Adulteress Faces the Light of the World

And everyone went to his *own* house.

But Jesus went to the Mount of Olives.

But early in the morning He came again into

the temple, and all the people came to Him; and He sat down and taught them.

Then the scribes and Pharisees brought to Him a woman caught in adultery. And when they had set her in the midst,

they said to Him, "Teacher, this woman was caught in adultery, in the very act.

"Now Moses, in the law, commanded us that such should be stoned. But what do You say?"

This they said, testing Him, that they might have *something* of which to accuse Him. But Jesus stooped down and wrote on the ground with *His* finger, as though He did not hear.

So when they continued asking Him, He raised Himself up and said to them, "He who is without sin among you, let him throw a stone at her first."

And again He stooped down and wrote on the ground.

Then those who heard *it*, being convicted by *their* conscience, went out one by one, beginning with the oldest *even* to the last. And Jesus was left alone, and the woman standing in the midst.

When Jesus had raised Himself up and saw no one but the woman, He said to her, "Woman, where are those accusers of yours? Has no one condemned you?"

She said, "No one, Lord." And Jesus said to her, "Neither do I condemn you; go and sin no more."

Then Jesus spoke to them again, saying, "I am the light of the world. He who follows Me shall not walk in darkness, but have the light of life."

PHILIPPIANS 1:6

Being confident of this very thing, that He who has begun a good work in you will complete *it* until the day of Jesus Christ.

This timely message from Jack Hayford is also available on audio tape and video cassette!

Titled "Where Have All the Flowers Gone?", it is available directly from Living Way Ministries Resources.

To order:

Audio tape—send $4.00 plus $1.00 shipping and handling plus applicable sales tax.
Video cassette—send $19.00 plus $2.00 shipping and handling plus applicable sales tax.

Please mention code number 3003 for either product and state whether you are ordering the audio or video tape. If you are ordering the video please indicate either VHS or Beta. Please remember to include your return address.

Mail your order to:

Living Way Ministries Resources
14480 Sherman Way
Van Nuys, CA 91405-2499